MENDING PATH AND SOUL

POEMS

MENDING PATH AND SOUL

POEMS

Gift Foraine Amukoyo

Soft Grid Limited

Gift Foraine Amukoyo

Published by

Soft Grid Limited

Plot 6, Block 23, Satellite Town

Calabar, Cross River, Nigeria

+234 (0)8027676550, +234 (0)8053110637

E-mail: softgridbooks@gmail.com

softgridltd@hotmail.com

www.softgridbookslimited.com

First Published in 2018

ISBN 978-978-56095-7-8

Soft Grid Books

First Printing, October 2018

Dedication

3

To people finding worth of themselves

To people finding worth of themselves

Phases in Places

In all of these places, such places
I wish I had never passed those phases
I am so missing those faces
Those faces in those places
Fazes faded in every facade

Bring back those faults, those face fall
I would feel them without any falter
Pile them neatly with no forfeit, no retreat
Furnace it with the heat in my heart
Forge it; I will not take an exception

It is in you; it is in me
Time has registered our roles
I only crave those phases
If I have to travel time tunnels
Funnelling the drips of destiny
Departing in vast plains
We must all triangulate those phases
And may never repeat those faces

I mirror a glimpse of those fleeting phases
Like a flashlight weakened by battery drains
Never to behold those faces in those places
Pictures did not tell lies in the days of yore
Far and near pictures now profess billions of falsehood

True faces, nature does not lie
Faces I see you in my heart
Do you crest me in your diary album?
Phases hold still so I could reminisce those faces
Let me romanticize the facelift in thousand seconds

My walls have ceased to be mine
My colours no longer my choice, I couldn't chance it
Faces have splattered shades on my reflection
You paint my love all beautiful and bold
And in all those phases with those faces

I enclosed and drummed on in likes and dislikes
Set more paces in success, I shall match your paces
I wish you successful phases, I pray thee Godspeed
I miss you, faces I wish I could still face
I love you all faces, thanks for heightening my pace

Happiness of My Palm

Feed off my hand, the fruits of my field
The little seedlings of my laborious palm
That is the honest love I have to share
I hope you would gladly feed off my sweat

Do not tell the world it is emblazed with
Sorrow and hunger
I do not give out of my abundance
But from the little of my love
I hope you would gladly lead off my living

I was given a soil out of love
Do not fear to take a bite from this soil of love
It bears no sort of sore
I have not poisoned the crop with my worries
Nor spiced the harvests with the aches of my mind
Only with the love of my heart have I offered you my love

Riches in Rags

To reform
I have to foil
A form to fill
This void of fullness
Empty in abundance
Of riches in rags
With wealth in wells
Cons coiled in coyness
With cranky can of cunning
Of maize amazed by the millet
The chickens scared of corn
The snake repulsive of its venom

Shrub of Hope

Caress my soul with your flawless spirits
Anoint my soul with your consecrated tears
Nuzzle my neck with your healing balm
Cuddle my mind with humming hands
Graze my thoughts with swimming knuckles
Hug my heart with alluring words
Grip me with soothing fists
My heart longs for you
My beating ears are dumb to you
My broken eyes are blind to you
They lead me through paths of howling clouds
My crooked feet are crippled to you
They walk me on treacherous grounds
Numb are my senses, they rile against you
My nose clogged arrows your fuelling breath
My tongue dry it tastes not your apple a day
But every day of physic nut sickens me with its flavour
I hale from irresistible fallowed prescriptions
Dish me your juicy herbal subscriptions
Juice me, juice me; inject it in my running veins
My mind and heart, body and soul
Grapples for your flowery bosom
Hold my hands, take my arm
String me up; I yearn for your fertile fatigue
I'm balled in, haunted by hounding hooves
Shield me from the decimating thuds
The hounds are at my feet
They hurry harder, pounding on my knees
The shrieking sound dusting my strength
Its bellowing sweat washes every ounce of my will
Fangs digging deep in my flesh
Hear me out here

My thoughts are slummed in murky waters
My resolve mocks my rescue
My distorted senses slumber in shabbiness
I seek solace in this shrub of hope
Let the thorns prick at my senses
Wake me up; let the flowers not fall on me
The soft roses of sweet scent would drug me deeper in sleep
And so in my weakness, I battle with strength
My struggle swims near the riverbank
Before I duck fully under water
The sun breezes in its solidarity and enriches me in light
My feet flap in the soothing water
Its flowing pureness tickles
The melody of its current on my feet

Sorrow

All I need is a whip to cane this sorrow
All I need are feelings to close this hollow
Of a sorrow that whips like an arrow
My desires are chained in this horror of lust
Of fleeting dreams and losses
With keen terror
I fear I am losing this battle

Friendly Fire

This is the point where we break
And have to go our separate ways
We are not saying goodbye, no
Choices have been made, destiny beckons
We will cross paths
Only to part once more
We could never again
Grace our very own presence
Such as those designed timings
If coincidentally our paths cross
We get to hold hands
But like a bird's feet grazing waters

Most days, I turn to share an idea with you
I look to my right, the space is void
It's no more you seated by my side
It's a familiar fragrance, yet not intimate
Not your facelift with beaming smiles
With creased brows, pondering
And digesting my innovation
When you trail it's all nonsense
Just so to allay fears
And lighten tense mood

I can still hear your wild laughter
So melodious, comforting
More a soothing balm
Being kindled to my flesh
Spiralling waves of relief

All those are now gone with the wind
Whisked to a place it can never be retrieved

I'm alone, not so alone
Tides worsened, as a glimpse
Of each other came a treasure

Then came a day
We battered words, words
Like hammers with which one blow
Drives a hundred-inch nail into a wall
I yearn for those sweet times together
But they can never turn clock

At long last, we had the warmest of contacts
A time to have made merry memories
It was the last day we would be at leisured pace
Wish ourselves words of goodwill
But we never did those
For whatever reasons

I cannot now fathom
We were so displaced
Wish I can take that back
But it what it was, still is
One thing I am glad
Is the good times surpassed the bad

Of which I hold dearly to my heart
Like a rose given to me by mine truly
I know that one day
On such rare occasions
The sun will shine as the rain drops
And the moon will play on our stars

Please Tell

What strange-familiar song would you have me write?
What lamentation lyrics would you have me right?
What crooked path would you have me straight?
Skating round, what is not prone to lit a dark street
The cloak of depression and despair a vain threat

The clock of uncertainty suffocates hope's territory
The luck of success shuts from the grip of mastery
The lock of prosperity miles from satisfactory
Patience is on the verge of collapsing in failure factory
Virtue is drowning, creeping in indignity sanctuary

Down the lane of dogged struggles
The path to success can carve many dirt roads
Strength sizzled, whispers to the weary jaw of hopes
Club the blows, trumpet of victory are at the bells
Sniffing rocks, stones and blocks

All are liquid obstructions
The mouth stifles cries of woe fare at its tail
No shadow, no reflection, sight flaunts a blurry path
But a bickering tunnel beckons in full length
With a brave heart, aura braced corridors

And from every wall, the torches flamed up
The ladder of success is not sturdy but faulty stairs
Give me the codes to patience, virtue needs it
Pass on the keys to wisdom, understanding craves it
What familiar song would you have me write?

What lit darkened street are you ignorant
You must pass tests by the border of greener pastures

You must entreat the tickets to take flights
Make a crawl, take a kneel
Take a bow and telegraph the heights

Make a lift and stamp your feet in readiness
Breathe, always breathe, and take a step,
Make a race; take a glance, tweet how far gone
So far, so good, look no further
Forward ever, backward never

If your feet carry you too slow, take a flight
Fly high, on high, borrow the ears of dolphins
Wear the shades of eagles, bear the wings of ostriches
So many lamentation lyrics in the coffers of success
What strength of songs would you have me sing?

Lightened or darkened streets orchestrated by switches
The clouds must give way for the
Moon, stars, and rains, brace
Fasten your seat belt for every flight,
The clouds have no choice
What more strength of songs can I write?

Spiral of Silence

The mind is thrown; the heart is balled
Only the deep can call to deep

I bare my wound; you dig a ditch
Only the deep can call to the deep

I whimper pains in muffled silence
You wail wild merriment in distaste
Only the deep can call to the deep

I am dip underneath water
I bubble in drowned suffocation
Only the deep can call to the deep

I heighten my evaporated speech
You throw pebbles on my babbles for sport
Only the deep can call to the deep

I sob my Tata tears, you dab
Handkerchief in the ocean and hang it to dry
Only the deep can call to the deep

I have pitfalls in my stockings, holes in my pockets
You fill my water in a basket
Only the deep can call to the deep

I propel positive
You ruffle negative
Only the deep can call to the deep

You cannot give what you do not have
You cannot take what you do not give

Only the deep can call to the deep

Do Tides Breathe?

In the space of twenty four hours
I saw life was just vanity upon vanity
The tropical wetness, a sloppy haven
Its desperate dryness squeezes the oil
Out of the coconut
And it becomes a whitish shaft
The unknown historic water guzzled in its warm cocoon
The floodgates of wind razes spasm of debris
Looking through the window
Frozen by those scurrying feet

In space of five seconds
I knew this life was vanity upon vanity
Motion figures, still photographs
Black out breathe out
Dust to dust, sand in mould

In the space of one second
Laughter which echoed like the jaws of Eden lapsed
In that very second
Chaotic feet danced the steps of joy
Trailed by melancholy roaring with sinister laughter
Upon the roof tops of joy, stranded
Gasping for breath, a heavy toll sweeping its refuge

Fan and Fire

Scarred from under the sun
Out in its thirsty heat
Its hungry breath exhales brimstone and
Starry I gaze at its glittering shininess

Scarred from under the sun
I dare to brace its blazing cauldron
I try to ward off its lighting terror
I am dulled to wage its slitting smokiness

The burning radiant rose of Sharon
Shines on, scorching my skin
Yet I cannot shield it from me
It heats my heart
My breath gasps for a parcel of it

I try to ward off its fire
But sun up sun down
Life is open to fan and fire
Sun down sun up
Life is bared to sadness and sweetness
The sun in its rays of ways lashes at every brow
Sunny sockets are on the roof of every head
For its season escape is of gold mine

What shield can wage the scabbard of the sun?
What ocean can sheathe the sword of the sun?
Longer you stare at the sun
Eyes aflutter
Blinking to blind

For its season

Laced with sour stinginess and soaring sweetness
Darts the skin as a snake with seven heads
Each pokes infiltrating pores to the sixth
Hell on one pole to the seventh heaven

Glory of Gut

What you administer to the heart
It ministers to the soul
The soul compounds the spirit
The spirit conforms to your grace
Grace confers on you
The glory of gut
To make great of grit

Set Sail

In wake of a tortuous journey
Bear in mind
With resilience your
Point of unburden
Would be a lap of luxury
Set sail like a ship
Bound for the ocean's depth
The tides would lure you
To a Treasure Island
And the waves
Will wave you back to shore
When you are unsure of landing

Trauma Dull

For God is with me on this seat
Woes cling to your garment, you fate of deceit
Cast not your lecherous smiles upon my lips
His stars and lights a bicker to my leads
Beckoning my tears and my anguish to light
Leading me to the King of heart
On a precious throne vast with my beloveds
Your name is chanted depression
Like I should hail you the Almighty suppressor
I will not be fooled
I know your traits are diced in deceit
A disguised pit made a bed of defeat
By the fall the body shatters in aftermath
Knowing it succumbed to a scum as you
You wretch of a soil I found my feet
I command control of my mind and body
For the keeper of my soul
It pleases Him to know I soar
My way to his ample bosom
Crested by my beloveds at his right

Wrath Is Not

When you vow your wrath
Hitting the ceiling, vengeance is of essence
By emotions you delude your worth
For it will burn you to rot
It upholds you to nought
As your heart becomes feed for hate
Black beast that consumes your soul
Digging a shallow memorial park
Arrows of bitter pills
Are injected into your veins
Solely your heart so ejects only anger
Smother those graves beautiful one
Your storm is just a puppy's cry
When it is not soothed
It sinks, soars and shatters to bruises
Transforming you to a needless wolf
Keep calm; whatever goes wrong
It does not soil your ego
If you offer love, peace
Than profess your wrath
Leading only to hurt
Your mind would wither to shaft
Rot upending your hurt
For wrath, its pleasurable orgasm is staged

My Muse

How I breathe without you is mythical
How I lived without you is a mystery
Potent are your jibes to my ribs
Magically your sorcery spirals
Down the graves of my mental retardation
Your presence cures me of my silence
You shock me deep in my numb shackles
Unbound I cue at your delicate tirades
Tie me to your amiable wrist
Ring me to your saucy waist
With you my spirit of scribbles awakens
On your tail my pen runs when it is jerked
And its ink turns like a crocodile dreary on its prey
A lion in its desperation is limitless
It dares to feed from the alligator's mouth

My muse is nestled in the lion's den
In my brash cowardice I shall dine within
For I must have my muse back to wine in me
On stages and pages
The poet is life and soul of the party
Using the LI-FI tone of an automated bard
The poet's word is life of Riley
His lines are life affirming
Some lyrics are written in the head
And never spoken with the mouth

Priceless Piece

Poetry is a priceless piece
Pleasantly principled
Powerful fluid of
Passionate penmanship
It is spellbinding and pacifying
A prescriptive pill
For every heartthrob
It is companionable for emotions
Poetry is so nourishing
Whenever and however dished
Juiced to placate every soul
Poetry is a pabulum
It is perpending
Poesie est puissant
Poesie gebeine pristnus

Trial by Fire

In my moment of trials
You stayed away from me like I had leaping leprosy
When it's tasty time, do well to stay
Further away like you would from a snake's spittle
If you come any closer
I will make you feel
That when a toothless new born
Nips hard at the mother's nipples
It sends ripples of shocks to her nerves
Connoting her brows to whiskers
While the inexperienced onlooker
Wonders how that is possible
In trying times, strangers can be more
Blood than water
Foes can be the best of friends
In trying times, a lot of awes strike you
Spell bound and disoriented
Tasty times can be tasteless
On the tongue of the sickly

Please do not flag down my tricycle
If you are stranded on the highway
It's best you ignore my headlights
If you insist, look at the seats
You can see they are occupied
By the disabled and the destabilized
Maybe if it had been a four wheel
They would be some space to fit you in
It could have been possible
But you deflated the fourth tire
You deprived me of a four-wheel
When you were in the right position

In my next turn per chance you're still here
I will bear in mind to reserve a quarter space
Don't call me mean; it's just the way it may be
In trying and tasty times, lots of shit surface
In trying times I pleaded with you to stay with me
In tasty times I dare you to move on without me

November Remember

November remember
When the weather is dizzy
It is fertile with a precious bloom
November remember
When the sun comes to cool
And the breeze turns alluring
A lover is playing blues with the flute
The moon listens with seduced heart
November remember
That which you will bear
Is a controversial powerful fruit
Frowned at, spit at, yet cherished
November remember
The birth is trailed with stars of wisdom
And the wise will merry with knowledge
November remember
To that which you have birthed
I shall bow down on my knees and adore
November remember
That I shall bear my treasured gold at your feet
Lay freshest of frankincense to fill
The air with aromatic fervours
And myriad of myrrh will flourish in the air
November remember
You are a great forerunner that fanned ember
Making its light shine forever
November remember
I reverenced in your presence
As the purest of all to conceive and birth this ember
November remember
You are the smoke that escapes from the fire
November remember

You are the usher of ember
November remember
You are always a chariot of December
November remember December
Daisy daintily defined

River Believer

I have always flowed with the river
Never to fall out of love with its maker
Slipping fever on your river I am a believer
Your flawless riverbank safety will deliver
Your meditating wave assures your finder
River moisture my soul, my heart drifts brighter
River you flow in my world you're a committed giver
With splashes of pureness, your grace never dither
My belief cries out river I am not your leaver
River, river how besotted I'm to your chandelier
Graciously your river has brazened my liver
Intricately a faithful weaver strings my vows filler
I solemnly vow not I your river waver
I wake in the river, my liver never quiver
The Psalms of the river songbirds my grieves taker
The Job of the river my courage beeper
River slushes succulently as my sublime anchor
In the river my heart joys with a heaver
In the river my fears vanquish with shiver
River, river, my joy flows free from Babylon River
The righteousness of the river resurrects the faith not of its leaver
My mouth tastes the flavours of this irresistible river

Elasticity of Life

At the realm of death
I see the soulless edges of life
The spring has slackened
The elasticity of life is fragile
The cold of the morgue is my bane
I would want to go home warm
Sleeping in my body cloth
Soulful screams have hounded my voice
Sleeping stitches have haunted my eyes
Show me the bed of roses to lay awhile
My maker must have greater roses
For me to lay and rest eternal

Call of the Sublime

These catastrophes have beautiful names
With sublime smiles
Serene Faces
Alluring feet
Wallowing in contorted toes
And polished nails

Carrying waves of stormy steps
Barking tones of stormy pace
Curving the love of Matthew and Harvey
In the uncanny season of their love
The aftermath of their pleasure has left
The world in orgasmic disarray

Hurricane Maria you have ceased to be mild
And become a brash reign of terror
A telephony storm of chaos
Hurricane Irma your feet of Jealousy is astounding
Jose is just a ruthless home breaker

In the wind of your pleasures
You have crumbled walls of joy
Lily Lee you are gone with your crooked knee
But your lashes have imprinted brutal sores
Deep sores so sour your depth of debt is deep

The hurricane wisp hard
All caned are buried in lapses
Memories buried in ashes
Your dust have razed our living and existence
Your fate is a stringer of our faith
Your face is a phase of horror

Life

Greatness comes in different trails
Wealth is served on different trays
The journey of life is conveyed on different trains
We reach destinations through several terrains
Some arrive in similar coaches
Lessons of life take us to many branches

Penholder

My bellybutton is my penholder
My words are born from the womb
My muse cuts off the umbilical cord
The ink of my pen is a mustard fluid
That will birth for ages and sages
The lyrical poems of my realm
The older my pen
The more gripping my lyrics

Silent Passover

He said his life would lapse in three years
Sadly
I never fathomed
It would be barely three days for
Three is an even
Years are an odd

Stupid me
I choked on my tears
When the news reached me today
I was left beaten with the shock
I am left battered with regrets
Of his silent Passover

He chose a time for his passing, it seems
He chose to make merry with neighbours
Little did I know he was holding his mourning eve?
A ceremony of anguish to languish in time
How did it elude anyone he wished not the
End of his missing ribs upon his demise

You should have tarried a little longer
All I wanted was to dive your corpse to the sky
Breeze your nostrils to the atmosphere of the air
I wanted your coffin to sit on the clouds for seasons
To be dry of crimsons
And socked with whitish firmaments
I did not want your passing to be of the earth
Farewell, smiling Angel
I see the laughter in your silent eyes
That you have reached the havens of your hymns

Impatient Clock

When his time was near
The withering man spoke in his dialect
When time hurried with a cane
The withering man leapt with his clan
The lash clashed on the clan
When the time came in handy
The withering man ate words of his mother tongue
When time came abreast of his belly
The withering man crawled on spiky foods
As time came burning
The withering man danced like a wavering tree
When grim reaper knocked like a neighbour
The heart of the withering man lapped
Like the lazy waves of the ocean

When the time was hair's breath
The withering man dug his bed
On the roughness of the earth

When time ticks cords of hauling soils
The withering man weeds and plants his harvest vest
The withering man mourns within a stone's throw
The withering man cushions his fall on thorns
When the time hums touching hymns
The withering man whistles like a lost bird
Its wings weak to wriggle or fly
His mind weak to smoke the craggy air

When the grim reaper is old and wise
We beat out tripod pots
Wear yards of triple white fires
When the grim reaper is young and prime

We roll out in blacks
We dark shade our emotions
Is it the cry of the owl?
That makes it an omen
A prophet of doomsday?
Is it its monstrosity that makes it calamitous?
Did its body make men spit spittle that galls its nature?
Amongst phenomenal creatures
What makes the grim reaper so repulsive?
Is it when it makes love cry
As you lay to rest
Withering man, as the grim reaper made a call
Know your clan laid siege to your vault

Break Strife

Break a knee
I will walk on still
My pace has become a steam
My strides have become savage
I will stamp on anything
I will match on steel
My heart has been ironed out
To walk on hills
And stamp on rocks
My feet do not feel any hurt

Break a tooth
I will speak on waves
My tone has become speechless
My voice sinister
I will sing in outrage
I will wail with fury
My tongue has been drenched in vinegar
To speak of sermons
And preach on pulpits
My vocals do not fear souls
My voice will be vulgar
To a distasteful level

Break a face
I will carry a picture
My image has become motionless
My mirror is a perfect reflection
I will telegraph any still picture
My vision has been circumcised
To sight any displeasure
And reminiscence on vintage

My eyes are gain strife to strife

Bloodless Heart

I found your heart outside your body
Saying no to the weakness of your soul
With a bloodless stain
I see the pains in your eyes
I curse the happiness behind it
Let the smiles making your pain
Be frozen in haste

The heart carries the burden
Of every clan
It has no family
It is a communal bard
That whispers no clashes of tone
An unconditional love
That brings peace to the world

Genes

My genes are strong
Naked and bathed in a stream of steam
My lineage is a baobab stem
They wobble on hale
They are not fickle
They shy off sickle
My mind is heartily fierce
It dabbles on thin fillers
I was never faint to crawl
I was weaned to walk on tides

I walked when it was barely time
Holey I am caged
In this splits of splitters
Splattering my stance
My stalks they store
Stunt they start
Of weakening my foundation
But I am a tree of stems
My genes are strong
I wobble on
Hale and hearty

Clipped

Clipping peg on linings
The world roams
Square peg in a round hole
The rainbows are made
Primary and secondary
The earth cannot fit into the moon
The stars cannot sit on the earth
Just as the creator made the snake and the lizard
Crawl in a world of beauty
Roses and thorns are bright and beautiful

Mayapple Mirage

I am growing up
So hard a tortoise shell
The pride in me never rests
In perfect peace
My peacock has sprung positivism
The day its feathers are plucked
That day my dignity is sold
It is not hubris
It is the charm which
Barricades my heart against hurt
From atrocities of evil importune

Smile saddens sorrow
Laughter lures life lace light
Jokes juggles joy
Hope glows amidst turmoil
Belief in oneself outweighs drums of criticism
The eyes shoot as far as the sight squints
The tongue can taste the pudding
By way of romanticizing
With the steaming aroma

The pulse of a heartbeat can be felt
With a palm placed to the bosom
A doctor and the thermometer is
A professional formality
Bleak beckons brightness
Darkness dies dastardly in daylight
Catastrophe caters calamity
Peace petals pelt prickling
Mild mind mars menace
Part peace paces in pieces

Caution curbs curses
Hoots hinders hunt
And the hunter becomes
The watched prey predator
You would have me plain and pliant
Weak and mush
Meekness has never held out milk to me
Do not intend to be soft now
I am springing in a harsh cove
I cannot succumb to feebleness

The Future Is Now

The future calls
That I be
For I think, therefore I am

I am boundless to the sky
I was born to fly
My dreams are on high

The future beckons
Your graceful nest has been
A worthy keeper

Of nature's haven
That nurtured my prime
That someday

I will flap my
Colourful wings
And poise to fly

Keep faith
My dreams do not sour
For If my wings are fractured

My knees may find
The ground a humble height
And floor my dreams

The future is now
Your counsels are my dreams tipper
They make my hopes stiffer

Wholly my dreams linger
As my heels hit solid grounds
Running on vast plains

Roaming joyfully to
Take unending flights
To reach for the stars

Drought in the Midland

Drought has flooded my eyes
Relief has beclouded my mind
I feel the pressure
Of the gates of mist
Its overpowering vapour
Has evacuated my peace
My peace has ceased to flow
Of this horror in a horrendous darkness
We gather fireflies in our palms
To lighten our way to doggedness
From claws that resonate in dirge psalms

Where Angels Dine

Where Angels dine
There I find a wing
In the abode of the birds
There I pitch my tent
To borrow a leaf
That falls from the tree house
As the melody of their flutes
Mesmerizes the flowery flowers
That cascade over my wings
Where rainbows commune
Paints the colour of my rest
That my peace comes after
The melancholy of my unrest

Passion

Tonight
Sleep eludes me as I think
That you can probably be an angel
Come to be with me awhile on earth
To guide and guard me
To care and cane my dreams
To a vision of realities
The clock says hurry
Your angel might not tarry
Longer than the appointed time
But there is a problem

Dear Angel,
I have fallen deep in love with you
I have broken the rules of heaven
I have defiled the ordination of mortality
And fallen deep in love with immortality
Affection so heavenly to my world
Of confections and sinful confessions

Your love is immeasurable
I have been to the ends of the world
In search of a tape roll to measure
The width and height of your love
But none I found in my long wait
Your love is immense
You immune me with devotion
My passion has become your passion

I wish I can reborn my birth
A birth cast off limbs and hinds
But with wings and crowns

Dear Angel,
I have seized your wings to fly
I have wrapped its feathery
Loveliness around my loneliness